WAYS INTO HISTORY

Florence Nightingale

Sally Hewitt

W
FRANKLIN WATTS

First published in 2004 by
Franklin Watts
96 Leonard Street
London EC2A 4XD

Franklin Watts Australia
45-56 Huntley Street
Alexandria, NSW 2015

© Franklin Watts 2004

ISBN 0-7496-5575-5

Series editor: Sally Luck
Art director: Jonathan Hair
Design: Rachel Hamdi/Holly Mann
Picture research: Diana Morris

A CIP catalogue record for this book is available
from the British Library.

Picture credits:
Photography by Ray Moller unless otherwise credited.
AKG Images: 10, 24t.
Bettmann/Corbis: 3, 18b.
Fotomas/Topham: 6.
John Frost Newspapers: 15l.
National Army Museum, London: 24cl, 24cr.
Peter Newarks's Pictures: front cover cl, br, 9, 14, 15r, 16l, 20.
Picturepoint/Topham: 12, 13, 16r, 18t, 26t, 27.
Pro Sport/Topham: 25l.
St Bartholomews Hospital, London/SPL: 7.
Science Museum London/HIP   Topham: 19, 22.
Sipa Press/Rex Features: 23.
Sotheby's/AKG Images: 11.
Richard Young/Rex Features: 25r.

Every attempt has been made to clear copyright. Should there
be any inadvertent omission, please apply to
the publisher for rectification.

Printed in China

Contents

Famous nurse

Florence Nightingale was born nearly 200 years ago, in 1820. She was a nurse who was famous when she was alive. She is still famous today.

Florence Nightingale, the nurse ▷

A nurse cares for people when they are hurt or sick. What jobs does a nurse do for patients in a hospital?

Nurses today do many of the same jobs that Florence Nightingale did then.

△ Nurses today

🔍 **Be a historian...**

Look carefully at the pictures of Florence Nightingale and of the nurses today.

What is different about them?

What is the same?

Florence grew up in a wealthy family. Children from rich families had lessons at home, not school. Only older boys went to school and university.

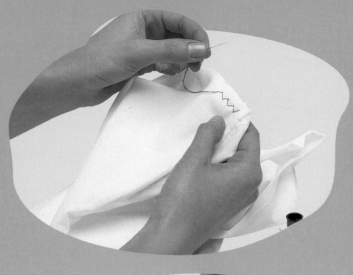

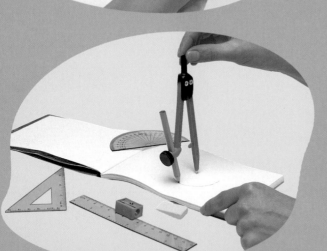

Girls were brought up to become good wives and mothers. Look at the pictures above. What lessons was Florence taught?

Florence was clever. Her favourite lesson was mathematics.

She loved reading books in her father's library.

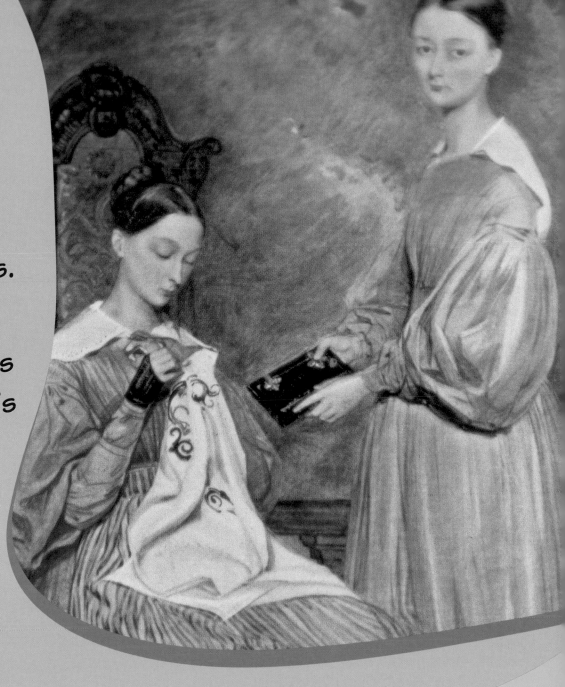

A portrait of ▷ Florence and her sister

Be a historian...
Do you think Florence enjoyed girls' lessons? Would you have enjoyed being a child in Florence's family? Why?

Growing up

Florence's family had lots of servants to work for them. There were cooks, gardeners, and nursemaids to look after the children.

A wealthy
Victorian
family ▷

💬 **Talk about...**

... what life was like for a wealthy married woman, like Florence's mother.

Use these words to help you:

husband   children   servants

parties   money   spare time

While Florence was growing up, she spent time visiting the poor and looking after the sick.

▽ Wealthy people taking food to the poor and sick

Florence enjoyed helping people. She decided not to marry. She would become a nurse instead.

Do you think her parents were pleased with this decision? Turn the page to find out…

Hospitals

Florence's parents didn't want her to work in a hospital. They said, "Nurses are like servants. They wash, cook and clean. Only poor people go to hospital!"

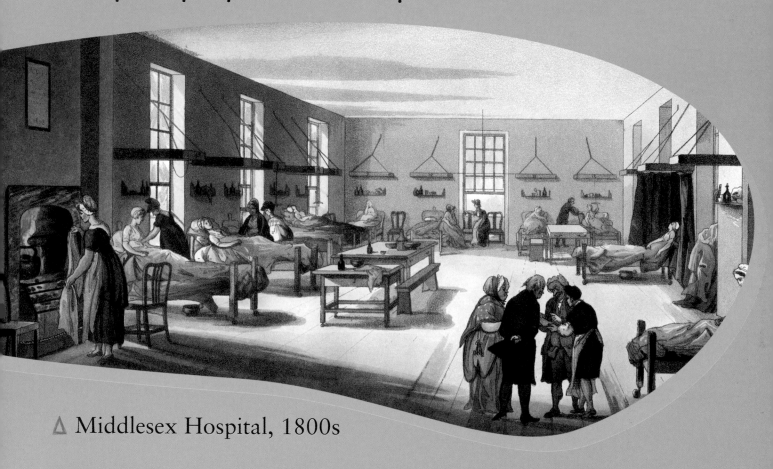

△ Middlesex Hospital, 1800s

Florence went to work in Middlesex Hospital. She nursed patients with cholera, which was a very dangerous disease.
What kind of person do you think Florence was?

Today, if you are ill, have an accident or need an operation, you go to a hospital like this one.

△ A modern hospital ward

🔍 Be a historian...

Look carefully at the two pictures.
Which hospital would you rather
be a patient in?
Can you say why?

The Crimean War

In 1854, Great Britain went to war with Russia. British soldiers were sent to fight in battles in the Crimea.

△ A battle in the Crimea

Soldiers rode on horseback. Their weapons were guns and swords. Many men were wounded in battle and became sick.

William Howard Russell was an eyewitness to the war.

That means he saw it happen.

He sent back reports to *The Times* newspaper in London.

William Howard Russell in the Crimea △

THE
WAR IN THE CRIMEA
THE OPERATIONS OF THE SIEGE.

[The following appeared in our second edition of yesterday :-]
(FROM OUR SPECIAL CORRESPONDENT.)
HEIGHTS BEFORE SEBASTOPOL, OCT 19.
The enemy scarcely fired a shot during the night of the 18th. Our batteries were equally silent. The French, on their side, opened a few guns on their right attack, which they had been working to get into position all night; but they did not succeed in firing many rounds before the great preponderance of the enemy's metal made itself felt, and their works were damaged seriously; in fact, their lines, though nearer to the enemies battles than our own in some instances, were not sufficiently close for the light brass guns with which they were armed. At daybreak the firing continued as usual from both sides. The Russians, having spent the night in repairing the batteries, nearly in the same position as ourselves,

◁ Article from *The Times*, 14 November 1854

🔍 Be a historian...

In one article, William Howard Russell wrote:

"Is it fit that the soldiers should suffer everything, and we nothing at all?"

What do you think he meant?

From London to Scutari

Back in London, Florence read the newspaper reports. Her friend Sidney Herbert was the Secretary of War. She wrote to him, offering to help.

△ Sidney Herbert

△ Florence Nightingale

At the same time, Sidney Herbert wrote to Florence asking her to help! They agreed she would go to work in a hospital at Scutari. How do you think Florence felt about her new job?

Florence set off on the long journey.
She took supplies and a team of 38 nurses.

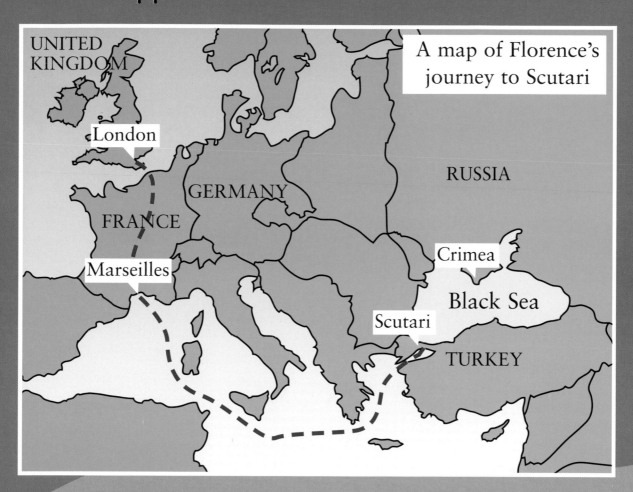

A map of Florence's journey to Scutari

UNITED KINGDOM

London

RUSSIA

GERMANY

FRANCE

Marseilles

Crimea

Black Sea

Scutari

TURKEY

Talk about...

... what Florence's journey to Scutari was like.

Use these words to help you:

| sea | land | boat | sail |
| train | long | time | distance |

What do you think she found when she
arrived at Scutari?

Turn the page to find out...

The wounded soldiers

△ The hospital at Scutari

The hospital at Scutari looked very grand from the outside. But Florence was shocked by what she found inside.

Wounded soldiers ▷

◯ Talk about...

... how the wounded soldiers felt.
Use these words to help you:
hurt   worried   afraid   pain   cold   hungry

Florence and her nurses worked hard to make things better for the soldiers.

The hospital after improvements ▽

🔍 Be a historian…

Look at the picture of the wounded soldiers and the picture of the hospital ward above. What changes did Florence make for them?

What do you think the soldiers thought of Florence? Turn the page to find out…

Lady with the Lamp

The soldiers loved Florence. Each night, she walked through the hospital with her lamp to say goodnight. They called her "the Lady with the Lamp".

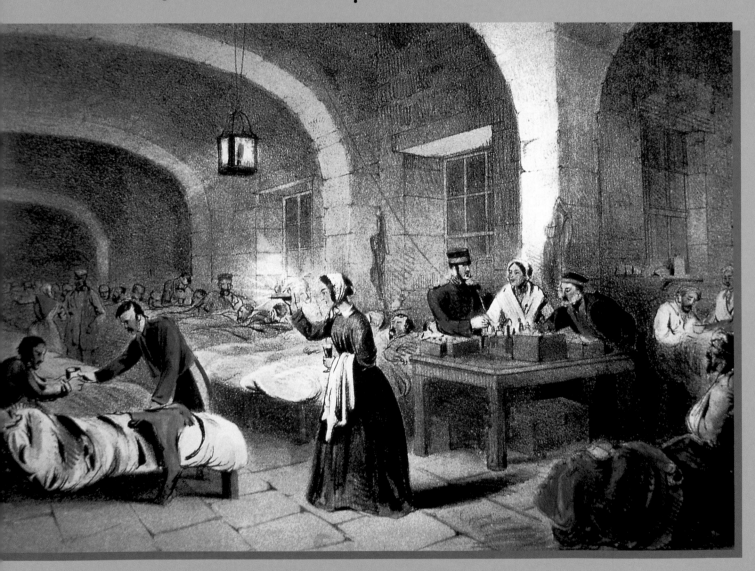

Why do you think the soldiers loved Florence so much?

Florence made sure the hospital was clean, warm and comfortable. She thought of things that would make the soldiers happy and help them to get better.

Dear Mother and Father

💬 **Talk about...**

... how Florence made things better for the soldiers.

Use the pictures to help you.

Raising help

Newspapers used pictures and reports to help raise money for the wounded soldiers. The money paid for food and supplies.

THE ILLUSTRATED LONDON NEWS [Feb. 24, 1855.

176

MISS NIGHTINGALE, IN THE HOSPITAL, AT SCUTARI.—(SEE PRECEDING PAGE.)

△ Florence at Scutari – from *The Illustrated London News*, 1855

⌕ Be a historian...

What supplies would Florence and her nurses need?

How do you think this picture helped to raise money?

Today, newspapers report on wars and other
disasters that happen around the world.
They often ask their readers to send
money to help the victims.

△ Earthquake in
Bam, Iran, 2003

Does your school send money to help others?
Do you think this is important?
What do you do to raise the money?

People at home read about Florence's work in the newspapers. They loved her for helping the soldiers. She was famous!

△ Queen Victoria

◁ The front of the brooch

The back of the brooch ▷

TO MISS FLORENCE NIGHTINGALE AS A MARK OF ESTEEM AND GRATITUDE FOR HER DEVOTION TOWARDS THE QUEEN'S BRAVE SOLDIERS, FROM VICTORIA R. 1855.

🔍 Be a historian...

Queen Victoria presented Florence with a brooch. What do you think the words on the back of the brooch mean?

What had Florence done to earn this reward?

Pop stars, film stars, athletes and politicians are just some of the people who become famous during their lifetimes.

Paula Radcliffe is a famous athlete

Nelson Mandela is a famous world leader

Talk about...

... these famous people.

What have they done to become famous?

Do you think they will still be famous in 100 years' time?

Why do we remember Florence Nightingale?

Florence returned from the war in 1856. She was famous but she didn't stop working.

Florence with nurses from her school ▷

Florence's book ▽

NOTES ON NURSING:
WHAT IT IS AND WHAT IT IS NOT.

In watching disease, both in private houses and in public hospitals, the thing which strikes the experienced observer most forcibly is this, that the symptoms or the sufferings generally considered to be unavoidable and peculiar to the disease are very often not symptoms of the disease at all, but of something quite different—of the want of fresh air, or of light, or of warmth, or of quiet, or of cleanliness, or of punctuality and care in the administration of diet, of each or of all of these. And this quite as much in private houses as in hospitals.

The process of repairing the body which Nature has instituted, and which we call disease, has been hindered by some want of knowledge or attention, in one or in all of these things, and pain, suffering, or interruption of the whole process sets in.

If a patient is cold, if a patient is feverish, if a patient is faint, if he is sick after taking food, if he has a bed-sore, it is generally the fault not of the disease, but of the nursing.

I use the word nursing for want of a better. It has been limited to signify little more than the administration of medicines and the application of poultices. It ought to signify the proper use of fresh air, light, warmth, cleanliness, quiet, and the proper choosing and giving of diet—all at the least expense of vital power to the patient.

It has been said and written scores of times, that every woman makes a good nurse. I believe, on the contrary, that the very elements of nursing are all but unknown.

By this I do not mean that the nurse is always to blame. Bad sanitary, bad architectural, and bad administrative arrangements often make it impossible to nurse. But the art of nursing ought to include such arrangements as alone make what I understand by nursing possible.

If we are asked, Is such or such a disease a restorative process? Can such an illness be unaccompanied with suffering? Will any care prevent such a patient from suffering this or that?—I humbly say, I do not know. But when you have done away with all that pain and suffering, which in patients are the symptoms not of their disease, but of the absence of one or all of the above-men-

She trained nurses at the Nightingale School of Nursing. She also wrote a book:
Notes on Nursing: What it is and What it is not

We remember Florence today for her brave work at Scutari. We also remember how she improved hospitals and nursing skills.

Nurses laying a wreath by the statue of Florence Nightingale in 1933 ▷

🔍 Be a historian...

Look back through the book.
Find examples of the changes Florence made for nurses and hospitals.

Why do you think we say Florence Nightingale's work "lives on"?

Timeline

1820
Florence is born in the city of Florence, Italy.

Start

1854
Florence starts work at Middlesex Hospital.

March 1854
Great Britain goes to war with Russia in the Crimea.

1855
Queen Victoria presents Florence with a brooch to honour her bravery.

November 1854
Florence arrives in Scutari with her team of nurses.

March 1856
The war ends.

August 1856
Florence returns to England.

1860
Nightingale School of Nursing is set up. Florence's book is published.

1910
Florence dies in London.

End

Glossary

Battle
A battle takes place when two enemy armies fight against each other.

Eyewitness
Someone who sees something happening with their own eyes.

Hospital
A building where people who are sick or wounded are cared for.

Nurse
Someone who looks after people who are sick or wounded.

Patient
A sick or wounded person who is looked after by nurses and doctors.

Report
A written account of something that has happened.

Secretary of War
A person who worked for the goverment and was responsible for the army.

Supplies
Food, drink and anything needed for getting work done.

Victims
People who are hurt or lose their home or family in a disaster.

Ward
A room in a hospital where patients are looked after.

Index